Back to School Coloring Pages Gift Book 1st Grade

Welcome Back to School Activities Book for Kids

Marko Dani

This Book Belongs To:

First Day
Coloring Pages

1st
Welcome Back!
1st

First Day
of School

First Day
of
1st
GRADE

Welcome to School!

Name: _______________________

Welcome to First Grade!

Official
First Grader: ________________

Author: ___________
All about Me...

Welcome to Second Grade!

Official
Second Grader: ___________________

Author: _______________

All about Me...

abc

© Rainbow Sprinkle Studio

Name _______________________

Name ______________________

Back to School

Animal Edition

Name:

____

Back to School
Name

a b c d e f g h i j k l m n o p q r s t u v w x y z
0 1 2 3 4 5 6 7 8 9 10
11 12 13 14 15 16 17 18 19 20
2 teach
A B C D E F G H I J K L M N O P Q R S T U V W X Y Z

LET'S
READ

paint
GLUE
CRAYONS

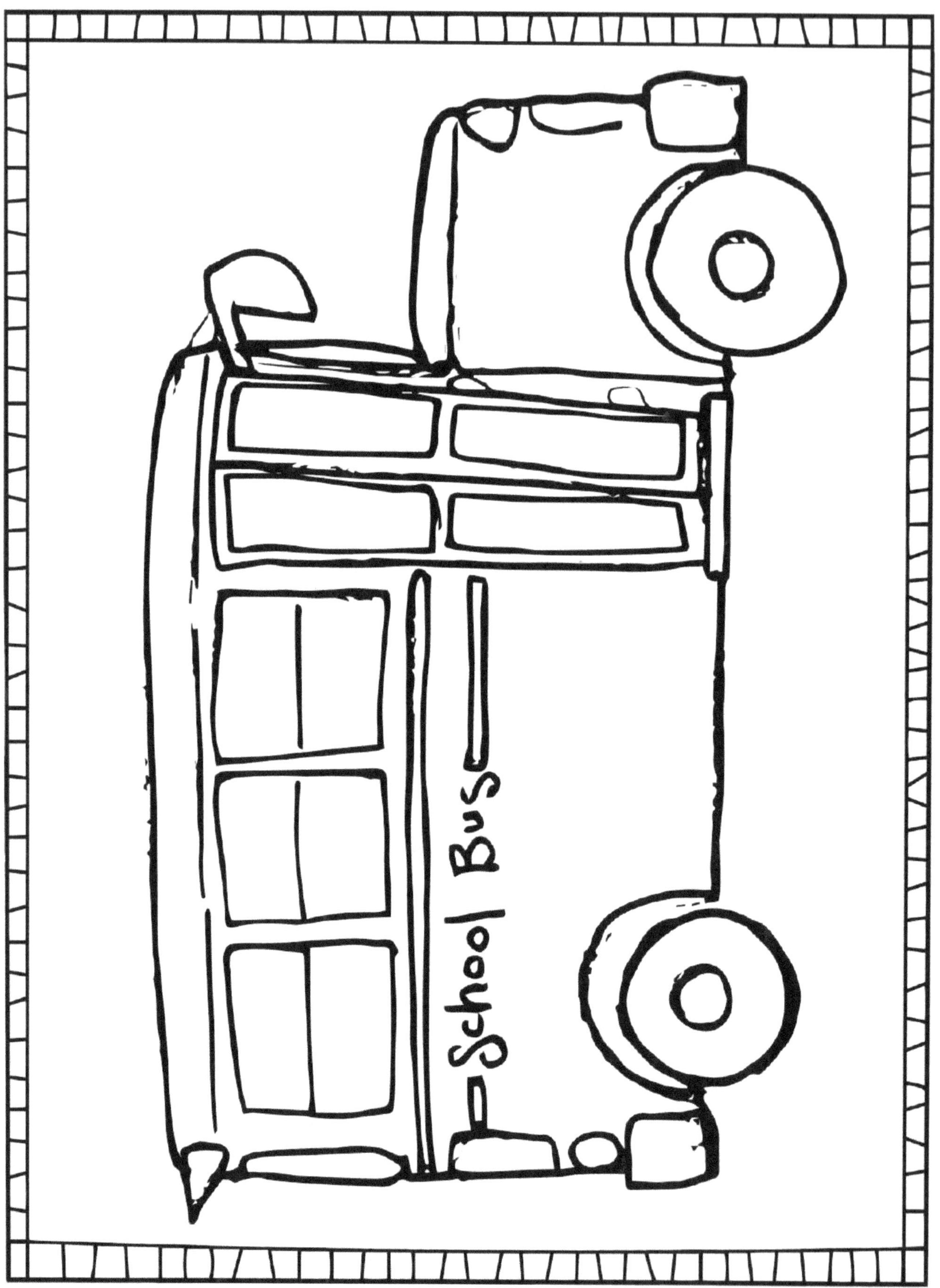

School Bus

School

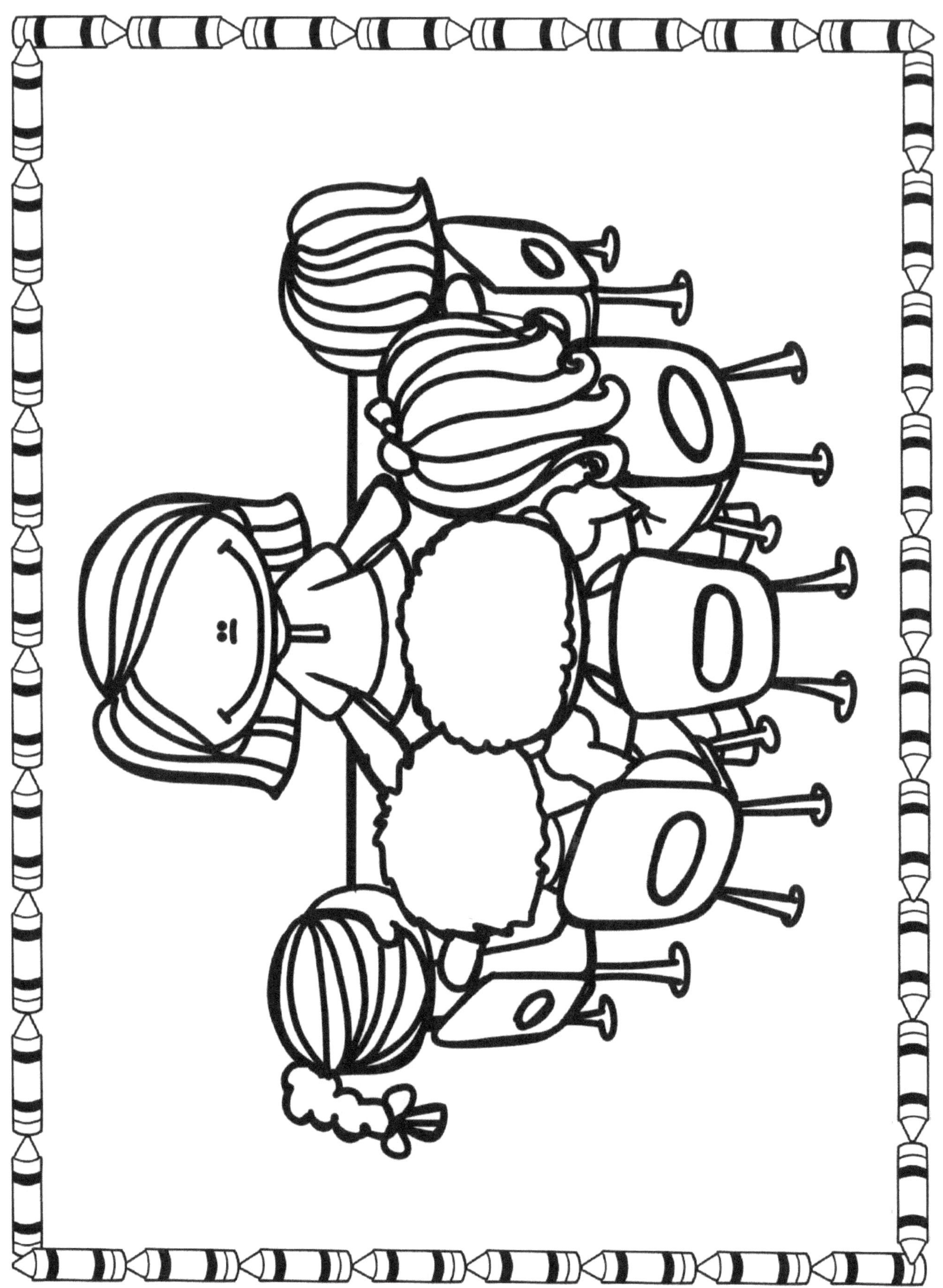

2+3=5

I ♥ MY STUDENTS

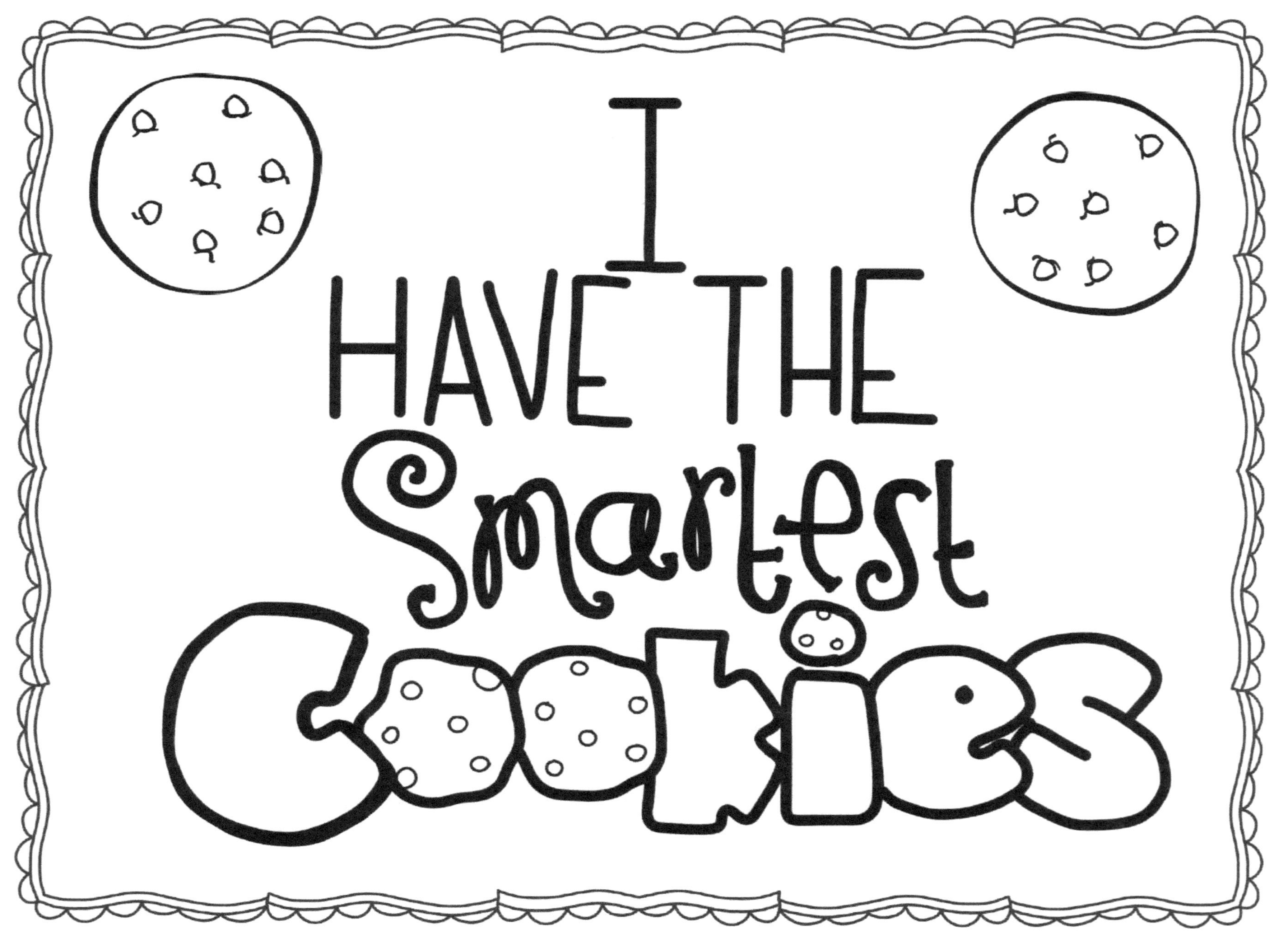

I HAVE THE Smartest Cookies

MY Students
Rock!

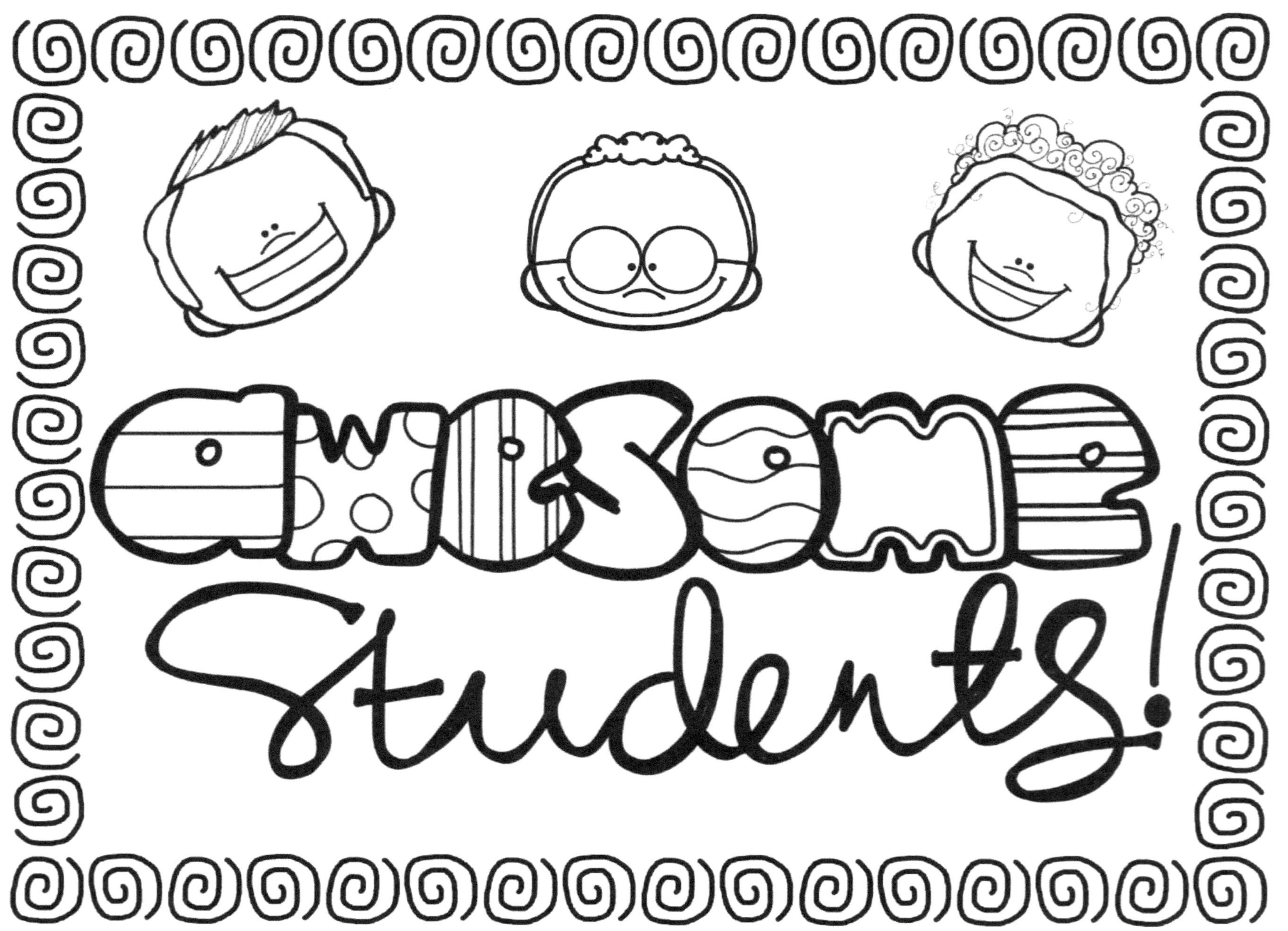

Awesome Students!